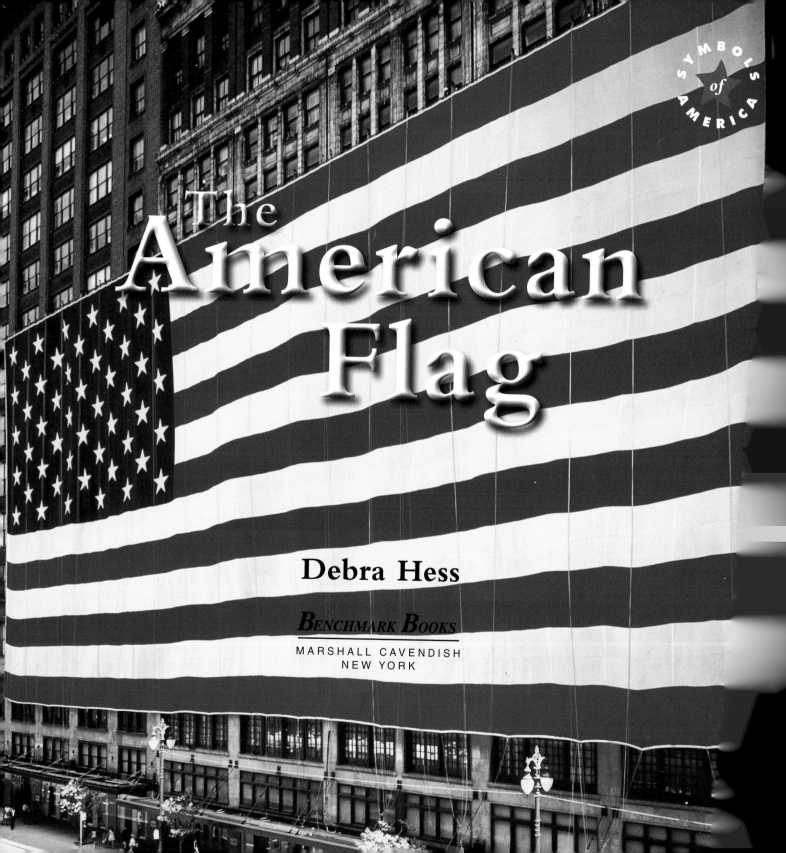

SYMBOLS of AMERICA

The American Flag

Debra Hess

BENCHMARK BOOKS

MARSHALL CAVENDISH
NEW YORK

Benchmark Books
Marshall Cavendish
99 White Plains Road
Tarrytown, NY 10591-9001
www.marshallcavendish.com

Library of Congress Cataloging-in-Publication Data
Hess, Debra.
  The American flag / Debra Hess.
      v. cm. — (Symbols of America)
Includes bibliographical references and index.
Contents: Stars and Stripes — The legend of Betsy Ross — Symbol of freedom.
  ISBN 0-7614-1709-5
 1. Flags—United States—History—Juvenile literature.
 [1. Flags—United States.] I. Title. II. Series: Hess, Debra. Symbols of America.

  CR113.H45 2004
  929.9'2'0973—dc21
                              2003004271

Photo Research by Anne Burns Images

Cover Photo by: Corbis/Ron Watts

The photographs in this book are used with permission and through the courtesy of:
Photri: title page, 4. Tom Raymond, 8, 16, 19, 24, 35. *Granger Collection:* 7, 12. *Corbis:* 11, 23, 31. Bettman: 15. Joseph Sohm: 28, Bob Rowan/Progressive Images: 32. *AFP/Beth Keiser Getty Images:* 20; Mark Wilson; Eliot Cohen: 27.

Series design by Adam Mietlowski

Printed in Italy

1 3 5 6 4 2

Contents

CHAPTER ONE

Stars and Stripes

"Shoot, if you must, this old gray head,
But spare your country's flag," she said.

These words from a famous poem by John Greenleaf Whittier are thought to have been *inspired* by an actual event. When the Civil War began in 1861, the South began flying its own flag. The North, however, did not remove the stars representing the Southern states from the American flag. It hoped that some day all the states would be united again.

During the war, *Confederate* general Stonewall Jackson marched his troops into Maryland, a *Union* state. They saw an American flag flying from the window of a house. When General Jackson ordered his troops to fire on the flag, an old woman stuck her head out the window and dared him to shoot. He decided not to.

◀ *A familiar sight—an American flag waves in the breeze off a front porch. But what if the flag looked different? What might it look like?*

The American flag stands for freedom and justice. Throughout the history of the United States, millions of Americans have died defending the flag and what it *represents*. In many countries around the world, people do not have freedom of speech. They cannot work in the jobs of their choice or practice the religion they believe in. Americans take pride in the liberties they are *guaranteed*.

Did You Know?

In 1831, shipmaster Captain Stephen Driver was about to leave on one of his many naval voyages. Some friends gave him a gift of a beautiful American flag with twenty-four stars on it. As the flag was flown for the first time, an ocean breeze lifted it into the air. The captain was so moved by the sight of the waving flag that he exclaimed, "old glory." The phrase stuck. Today, many people still call the American flag Old Glory.

▶ *This famous photograph shows American soldiers raising the flag on Iwo Jima, a Japanese island, during World War II.*

Before the American Revolution, each colony had its own flag or banner. After the revolution, the colonies decided they wanted to become a new nation, free from Great Britain. The revolution was fought for this reason. George Washington ordered the first American flag to be raised on January 1, 1776, on a hill near Boston, Massachusetts. It was called the Grand Union flag. It had thirteen red and blue stripes, but there were no stars. Since the colonies were not yet free, the crosses of Saint Andrew and Saint George—the symbols of Great Britain— were also on the flag.

◀ *In 1777, this was the design of the American flag. No one knows what the first flag really looked like.*

After the signing of the Declaration of Independence, Americans wanted their own flag. On June 14, 1777, when the United States of America was less than a year old, Congress passed a resolution that read:

Resolved: that the flag of the United States be thirteen stripes, alternate red and white; that the union be thirteen stars white in a blue field, representing a new constellation.

Did You Know?

• White is the color of purity and innocence.

• Red is the color of *hardiness* and *valor.*

• Blue is the color of *vigilance, perseverance,* and justice.

The American flag has been an inspiration to countless people. Here, Francis Scott Key sees the flag from aboard a ship and is inspired to write "The Star-Spangled Banner."

The new law did not say how big the stripes had to be or where the stars were to be placed. It said nothing about the design. It did not even state how big the flag should be. As a result, flag makers were free to make the flag look however they wanted. It wasn't until forty-one years later that Congress said that the stripes had to be *horizontal*. In 1912 President William Howard Taft signed an *executive* order that specified the *proportions* of the flag and the arrangement of the stars and stripes.

◀ *United States President William Howard Taft (1857–1930)*

CHAPTER TWO
The Legend of Betsy Ross

Many people think Betsy Ross made the first American flag. But history tells us that while Ross may have sewn a later version of the flag, she did not make the first official flag of the United States.

Betsy Ross was a Philadelphia seamstress who *embroidered* George Washington's shirt ruffles and sewed many other clothes for him. According to legend, when Washington became the general of the Continental Army, he gave Betsy Ross a piece of paper with a sketch of a flag on it and asked if she could sew it.

The colors of the flag stand for ideal characteristics, such as valor, perseverance, and justice. ▶

This story was first told in 1870 by Betsy Ross's grandson, William J. Canby. It was ninety-four years after the meeting between Washington and Ross supposedly took place. Historians have searched for proof that this meeting really happened. They searched in government records, diaries, and the writings of George Washington and others. No proof was ever found.

So who did make the first American flag? No one knows for sure. But historians think a man named Francis Hopkinson designed it. Hopkinson, a signer of the Declaration of Independence, was a member of the Continental Navy Board in 1776. It is believed that he began designing the flag of the United States during this time.

◀ *George Washington (sitting) meeting with Betsy Ross*

In 1780 Hopkinson wrote a letter to the heads of the Continental Navy Board. In this letter he said that he had designed "the flag of the United States of America," as well as several seals, ornaments, and checks. Hopkinson had never been paid for this work, and he sent along a bill asking if he could receive a "Quarter Cask of the public wine." In the eighteenth century, people were often paid for their services with food or wine.

Francis Hopkinson, who signed the Declaration of Independence in 1776, was also a New Jersey congressman. Could he have designed the first American flag as well? ▶

The board sent the letter and bill to Congress. Congress sent the bill to the Chamber of Accounts, which sent it to the Treasury Department. Over the next year, Hopkinson was asked to submit several new bills, and the matter was passed from the Treasury to Congress to a committee. Eventually, the Treasury decided that Hopkinson was only one of many individuals who had ideas and designs for the new flag. They paid him nothing. But the journals of the Continental Congress state very clearly that Francis Hopkinson designed the first American flag.

Schoolchildren across America say the Pledge of Allegiance to the flag every morning.

Did You Know?

The Pledge of Allegiance to the flag was written in 1892 by Francis Bellamy. He worked for a children's magazine and was working hard to make October 12 a national holiday called Columbus Day. The Pledge of Allegiance was said for the first time on Columbus Day in 1892 by 12 million schoolchildren across America.

21

CHAPTER THREE

Symbol of Freedom

Over the years, the flag has been redesigned and resewn many times. The original thirteen alternating red and white horizontal stripes remain. But as the United States grew from thirteen states to forty-eight, the flag had to be changed. By 1865 the flag had thirty-six stars. By 1912 it had forty-eight stars.

The forty-eight-star flag was in existence longer than any other. During the forty-seven years in which that flag flew, eight different presidents were in office. In 1959 Alaska and Hawaii became the forty-ninth and fiftieth states of the United States of America. When this happened, a boy named Robert Heft became famous.

The American flag has changed over the years. Here are three different historical designs: as it was proposed in 1777 (top left), as it was approved in 1794 (top right), and as it was changed in 1818 (bottom). ▶

"When I was in school, I was really shy," Robert Heft told a reporter from the United Press International news service in 1988. "I was always the type of kid to sit in the back of the class."

In 1958 Heft was in school in Lancaster, Ohio. At the time there were forty-eight American states. But everyone was talking about whether Alaska and Hawaii would become states. As part of a school project, Heft designed a fifty-star flag. He spent twelve-and-a-half hours one weekend arranging and sewing the stars. His mother would not help him because she was afraid her son was *vandalizing* the flag.

◀ *Heft's design replaced this forty-nine-star flag.*

Heft's teacher gave him a B minus. Heft thought he deserved a better grade. His teacher said he would give Heft a better grade if the student could get Congress to accept the design. Heft sent his design to his congressman.

Today, the original flag that Heft made is old and dirty. The colors have faded, but this famous school project has at one time or another flown over every state capitol building and eighty-eight United States embassies. It is also the only flag in America's history to have flown over the White House while five different presidents lived there.

The American flag flying over the Capitol in Washington, D.C. ▶

When folding the flag, no part of it should touch the ground. The flag is then folded into the shape of a tri-cornered hat, like the hats worn by colonial soldiers during the War for Independence. The red and white stripes are finally folded under the blue field.

Did You Know?

There is a United States Flag Code that tells you how to display the American flag. Here are some key rules, taken from Title 4, Flag and Seal, Seat of Government, and the States, of the United States Code Chapter 1, The Flag:

- The flag should be hoisted briskly and lowered ceremoniously.
- The flag should be displayed during school days in or near every schoolhouse.
- The only time the flag may be flown upside down is in a time of very great danger, such as war.
- The flag should not be displayed on days when the weather is inclement (bad), except when an all-weather flag is displayed.
- The flag should never touch the ground.
- The flag should never have anything added or attached to it.
- In the United States, no other flag may be flown higher than the American flag, except at the United Nations headquarters in New York City.
- A worn out flag, when it is no longer a fitting emblem for display, should be destroyed in a dignified way, preferably by burning.

On August 3, 1949, President Harry Truman signed a bill making June 14 of every year national Flag Day. On that day across the nation, Americans fly their flags. In this way, Americans show they are proud to be citizens of the United States. The American flag even flies in some unusual places, such as the North Pole, at the top of Mount Everest, and even on the Moon!

Astronaut John W. Young salutes the United States flag as he leaps on the surface of the moon in 1972. ▶

When an act of terrorism toppled the two towers of the World Trade Center in New York City on September 11, 2001, Americans looked to their flag for unity. Firefighters raised a flag amid the *debris* and *devastation*. The flag immediately became America's symbol of hope and endurance. Some people saw the flag and were reminded of the famous photograph of soldiers raising the flag at Iwo Jima during World War II. Some people even compared seeing the flag at Ground Zero to the sight of the flag that inspired Francis Scott Key to write the National Anthem.

◄ *An American flag is raised in the rubble of the World Trade Center as rescue workers look for victims after September 11, 2001.*

The flag will always be a symbol of liberty and pride during good times and bad. It remains the most recognizable symbol of America—a nation that fought to create a way of life different from anywhere else in the world.

A little girl waves the American flag proudly during a parade. ▶

Glossary

Confederate—Having to do with the Confederacy before and during the United States Civil War. The Confederacy was a group of eleven states that declared it was independent from the rest of the United States.

constellation—In the American flag's case, a pattern of stars that represents a group of states.

debris—The remains of something broken or destroyed.

devastation—Chaos, disorder, or helplessness brought about by a violent action.

embroider—To sew a picture or design onto cloth.

executive—The branch of government that carries out the laws of the United States.

guarantee—Anything that makes an outcome or condition certain.

hardiness—Having strength or nerve.

horizontal—Flat and straight across.

inspire—To influence and encourage.

perseverance—The quality of never giving up.

proportion—The size or dimensions of something.

represent—To serve as a sign or a symbol.

Union—The states that stayed loyal to the federal government during the American Civil War.

valor—Heroism.

vandalize—To destroy or damage property.

vigilance—To be alert or on the lookout.

Find Out More

Books

Herman, John. *Red, White, and Blue: The Story of the American Flag.*
New York: Grosset and Dunlap, 1998.
Quiri, Patricia Ryon. *The American Flag.* Danbury, CT: Children's
Press, 1998.
Ryan, Pam Munoz. *The Flag We Love.* Watertown, MA: Charlesbridge
Publishing, 2000.

Web Sites

Ben's Guide to U.S. Government for Kids
http://bensguide.gpo.gov

The Betsy Ross Homepage
http://www.ushistory.org/betsy

Index